D0034472

A PERILOUS PATH

A PERILOUS PATH

TALKING RACE, INEQUALITY, AND THE LAW

Sherrilyn Ifill,
Loretta Lynch,
Bryan Stevenson, and
Anthony C. Thompson

THE NEW PRESS

NEW YORK
LONDON

Requests for permission to reproduce selections from this book should be mailed to: Permissions Department, The New Press, 120 Wall Street, 31st floor, New York, NY 10005.

Published in the United States by The New Press, New York, 2018
Distributed by Two Rivers Distribution

ISBN 978-1-62097-395-0 (hc)
ISBN 978-1-62097-396-7 (e-book)
CIP data is available

The New Press publishes books that promote and enrich public discussion and understanding of the issues vital to our democracy and to a more equitable world. These books are made possible by the enthusiasm of our readers; the support of a committed group of donors, large and small; the collaboration of our many partners in the independent media and the not-for-profit sector; booksellers, who often hand-sell New Press books; librarians; and above all by our authors.

www.thenewpress.com

Book design and composition by Bookbright Media
This book was set in Caslon 540 and Oswald

Printed in the United States of America

10 9 8 7 6 5 4 3 2 1

Contents

Preface

In early 2017, New York University School of Law launched the Center on Race, Inequality, and the Law—a center founded on the idea that lawyers today cannot fully understand the American legal landscape without studying the relationship among race, ethnicity, and economic inequality on one hand, and the successes and failures of legal structures on the other. The center created a formal home for scholars who shed light on the interplay between racial politics and law in the United States, carrying on the tradition of NYU's own Derrick Bell.

To mark the founding of this center, I asked Loretta Lynch, former attorney general of the

United States; Sherrilyn Ifill (an alumna of NYU Law), president and director-counsel of the NAACP Legal Defense and Educational Fund; and NYU professor of clinical law and executive director of the Equal Justice Initiative, Bryan Stevenson, to join me for a conversation on February 27, 2017—about one month into the presidency of Donald Trump. I felt that the discussion was so insightful that it would be unfortunate to limit its audience to those who were lucky enough to be in the overflowing auditorium that night. So, in edited form, it is reproduced in this book.

—Professor Anthony C. Thompson, founding faculty director for the Center for Race, Inequality, and the Law at NYU School of Law

A PERILOUS PATH

Tony Thompson: So, we face the painful reality that we're headed down this perilous path. The toxic rhetoric over the last year has surfaced attitudes that we thought were confined to our history. We're experiencing a steady and dangerous marginalization of immigrants, people of color, and the poor. We're witnessing an uptick in hate crimes and hate speech. We're seeing government officials issue policies propelled by the twin forces of arrogance and ignorance. And we can't simply stand still and hope things will go well. We must take action, individually and collectively, to change the entire discussion of a nation. So, we're here to redirect a base, insensitive, and destructive national public conversation. We're here to reorient a country that seems to have lost its way. To paraphrase Dr. King's letter from Birmingham jail, we're here because injustice is here. We have work to do.

Many of the events of the last year have shaken us, but to a certain extent they were inevitable. We were not as vigilant as we should have been, and we became a little complacent over the last eight years. Recent events have reminded us that we need to regain our vigilance, and we must take on the challenge of justice at every turn. People in their twenties and early thirties have known eight years of an administration that embraced many of our values, and reflected our diversity, and advanced our ideals. So the tone and the conduct of this new administration are jarring. An important conversation is taking place for the heart and soul of America. And we must take the country to task where it must be taken to task.

We know that injustice and inequality often track along racial lines. Racism is embedded in the DNA of America. But while people of color have disproportionately felt its effects, it's an American problem. In fact, it is *the* American problem. And addressing it will require a collective strategy involving all Americans. As we witness the early decisions coming from this White House and this Congress, it has become apparent that the work on social justice will need to take place on two main fronts. The first being at the federal level, because we can't write off the federal government. The second will be at a local level, where we need to hold the line on progress and look for ways to make gains.

I want to talk for a minute about the local level. We're already witnessing progressive cities and states carving out spaces separate from the federal government. We have cities reaffirming their commitment to serving as sanctuary cities, and developing policies to direct local officials to defy ill-conceived, irrational, and unjust immigration holds. But that's just the beginning. Cities and states will have to become incubators for innovation. Local governments will have to develop novel approaches to reimagine and rebuild our democracy from the ground up. This means cities will need to find innovative ways to include rather than exclude the voices of people who are affected by these policies. Cities and states will need to develop new ways to build healthy communities. These efforts include new approaches to developing affordable housing, to placing critical mental and health care services in the neighborhoods where they're needed, and to investing resources toward infrastructure to better connect communities that continue to experience the effects of hyper-segregation.

We also will need to look to help communities continue their important work in the oversight of our police departments. We are already hearing a narrative of fear and misdirection and claims that crime is out of control—a narrative that justifies a path to a certain kind of law and order. Notwithstanding that crime rates are down in the country, they're looking to resurrect stop-and-frisk, and return to policies we have not seen since the war on drugs. We must resist that. We are seeing executive orders that, both in their tone and their optics, suggest that communities are to blame for the dire state of police-community relations. And we're seeing calls for reduced regulation and oversight of law enforcement. The challenge of today's generation has never been so clear. You've got to draw a line in the sand around inclusion, equity, and justice. We have work to do.

As the son of a Central American immigrant, I'm personally offended by a government that looks to exacerbate divisions rather than nurture and build our rich diversity. But being offended is not enough. I learned that lesson early in my career from two individuals on whose shoulders I stand: Professor Charles Ogletree and Professor Derrick Bell. Charles Ogletree was recently honored by the NAACP Image Awards for his lifetime commitment to justice. He taught me how to be a fierce advocate: he showed me how to speak truth to power when he represented Anita Hill in the Clarence Thomas confirmation hearings. And he found ways to fight for justice.

And then there's Derrick Bell, another mentor and a friend, who helped fight many of the critical battles while he was at the NAACP Legal Defense Fund. He also made it his personal battle to wage war on the lack of diversity in law school faculties.

In our conversation today, I don't want to focus too much on the administration, even though so much is happening daily. Sherrilyn, let me begin with you. When we think about issues of race and inequality, what are your concerns when you see a cabinet that doesn't reflect our rich diversity, and when you see the unpredictability in the White House these days?

Sherrilyn Ifill: This is a tough day to ask me that question, because just a few hours before I arrived, our associate director counsel Janai Nelson was on her way to Texas to argue part of our challenge to Texas's voter ID law—the most stringent voter ID law in the country, enacted after the Supreme Court's decision in the *Shelby* case.[1] This is the law that prevents our client, a university student, from using her university ID to vote. It prevents Native Americans from using their tribal ID to vote, and it prevents the use of all kinds of employee IDs that had been utilized in the past. Yet it *does* allow you to use a concealed gun carry permit as ID. (You just have to love Texas!)

This law has the effect of disenfranchising six hundred thousand eligible voters. And the Department of Justice, under Attorney General Lynch, and before that under Attorney General Holder, was co-counsel with us on that case. We challenged both the effect, under the Voting Rights Act, of that law, and the intentional discrimination that we believed formed the basis of

---

1. In 2013, the United States Supreme Court, in *Shelby County v. Holder*, invalidated the Voting Rights Act's key provision, which had put in place federal oversight to prevent states from enacting racially discriminatory voting measures.

that law.[2] We had won that case in three different courts on this question of whether it violates the Voting Rights Act because it has discriminatory effects, and we were sent back down to the district court to look at intentional discrimination. So we're arguing that case tomorrow morning. But just a few hours before I came, we received word from the new-and-not-improved Justice Department that they will no longer pursue and prosecute the intentional discrimination portion of that case with us.

This is not a surprise. We know who Jeff Sessions is, and certainly the Legal Defense Fund has known him for a very long time. It was our clients that he prosecuted in 1985 for voter fraud, in Perry County, Alabama. So we've known him for a long time, and this is kind of

2. The Voting Rights Act of 1965 prohibits racial discrimination in voting. The law describes its purpose as "ensur[ing] that the right of all citizens to vote, including the right to register to vote and cast meaningful votes, is preserved and protected as guaranteed by the Constitution."

what you expect. And yet, nevertheless, it kind of does take your breath away.

And I would have to say, in answer to the very specific question that you asked when you talked about a cabinet that doesn't look like us and doesn't look like America, I'm just happy about that. Because I actually was encouraged by the difficulty that this president seemed to have in finding qualified people to serve. I'm not interested in diversity in this cabinet, to be honest, given the positions that it was clear this president was going to take. So we're just at a very important flux moment for this country. Maybe a moment like no other. I've talked to a million people who say, we've been through this before, we'll do it again. And we've been through a lot of it before, but I'm not sure it's been quite like this, in terms of who's in the White House, and what I would call "the velvet rope" that has been removed from the shame, or what *used* to be the shame, of being racist, of being misogynistic. Even if you had those feelings, you tried to cover it. Now it's kind of out there. And so I think that's something very difficult to grapple with—the normalization of things that had been forbidden. And that's the world that many young people today will inherit.

Tony Thompson: Loretta, let me ask you. You were able to elevate issues of race and equal justice while you ran the Justice Department. These not only became part of the national dialogue, but also became part of the Justice Department's policy, and policy agenda. What are your concerns when you look at the role of government in these conversations about race?

Loretta Lynch: I think the example that Sherrilyn just gave really encapsulates the current situation and the challenge going forward. Because we are definitely in challenging times. A lot of things so many of us fought for are being deliberately and actively rolled back, trampled on. But what you're really seeing, which we have not seen in fifty years, is the peeling away of the role of government––the move away from protecting the disenfranchised, the move away from speaking to those who don't have a voice, the move away from lifting up people who have been pushed down, and the move toward being a participant in all of that.

And that's something that this generation has not seen. Many of us haven't seen it in our remembered lifetime. Our parents remember it. They remember it very, very well. Because there have been, sadly, periods in American legal life and American legal history when the law has been used to hold people down, to discriminate, and to harm our citizens. And so we thought we had moved away from that, because we had people who were using the law in a certain way. And the lesson is, how the law is managed depends very much on whose hands it is in.

So we have a situation where the Department of Justice steps away from one of the clearest examples of intentional discrimination, from the evidence that was educed in that case—and this is in the record, this is public—statements about not wanting certain types of people, or certain political views, to vote; this is the antithesis of America, I would say. Then you ask, who's left here to fight this? And I think we're at a point where the importance of organizations like the Legal Defense Fund is highlighted like never before. I mean, essentially, the Defense Fund has always been there, holding the federal government's feet to the fire. But you ultimately did gain a partner in the Justice Department. Now that partner has stepped away, and you will be in the forefront of this argument tomorrow and in the strategy sessions going forward.

We also see the importance of centers where you can have policy discussions with people from all walks of life, all generations, about how to craft policy. And I do think the local level is key here. The importance of the individual voice cannot be overstated. The only way we were able to get achievements in the first place, were individuals who came together and stood up and spoke out, at a time when they thought they could never win. The plaintiffs in *Brown* never thought they were going to win that case. That's just the reality of it. And then things came together in a way that allowed them to do so, and we've built on that. Now all of that is being unraveled.

Well, we still have those same people, who are going to be undergoing those same deprivations of law, liberty, and rights. And it's going to be individuals feeding into the groups that have always been the bulwark that I think are going to have to be the engines of change and thought in these issues and areas.

Tony Thompson: Bryan, with the exception of federal courts, the branches of federal government and many state governments are largely in the hands of those ideologically aligned with the administration. Given that, in what specific areas can those who are concerned about racial justice and inequality look to gain ground over the coming years?

Bryan Stevenson: I think we're going to have to focus on some things that we've not focused on. And I think it's partly looking at what federal government can do. It's also looking at what local governments can do. But I think we have to transcend even those institutional frames. For me, the challenge that we face is a narrative battle. I don't think we've actually done very effective narrative work in this country. We had a genocide in America. When white settlers came to this continent, they killed millions of native people, through famine and war and disease. And we forced those people from their lands. We kept their names. We named streets and buildings and counties and things after them, but we forced them off. And because of a narrative shift, we didn't say, "That's a genocide." We said, "Those people are savages." And that narrative failure to own up and acknowledge their humanity allowed us to think that we hadn't done anything immoral. But we did.

And then we had slavery and the Civil War.

The North won the Civil War, but the South won the narrative war. The South was able to persuade the United States Supreme Court that racial equality wasn't necessary. And they actually reclaimed a racial hierarchy, that ideology of white supremacy. And we allowed that to happen for a hundred years. Then we had horrific terrorism and violence. We ended the mass lynchings with impunity, but those who perpetrated that terrorism and violence won the narrative war. They were never held accountable. And then we got into the Civil Rights Era, where there was this massive, incredible movement led by extraordinary people, like Dr. King and Rosa Parks. We won passage of the Voting Rights Act; we won passage of the Civil Rights Act. But we lost the narrative war.

The people who were holding the signs that said "segregation forever," and "segregation or war," they were never forced to put down those signs. They didn't wave them around anymore, but they kept adhering to that value. And now we're living at a time where that thriving narrative of racial difference, that ideology of white preference, has exhibited itself, and now we're dealing with the consequences of that. We won an election in 2008, but we lost the narrative battle. We actually allowed that president to be demonized and victimized and marginalized because he's black—not because of anything he said or did. And our comfort with that kind of demonization is, I think, at the heart of the challenge that we face.

So, I want us to be engaged in legal battles in court. I want us to be thinking strategically, politically, about how we claim federal government *and* make local government work for us. But we've got to start fighting a narrative battle. We've got to create a country and a culture where you are not allowed to say, "I'm going to ban people because they're Muslims," and win with that. You're not allowed to ban people.

There will always be people who try to exploit the fear and anger that give rise to these kinds of narratives of racial difference. And I think we haven't done a very good job. Too many of us have taken advantage of the legal battles while leaving behind the narrative battle. And that for me is the great challenge that we face.

Sherrilyn Ifill: I think Bryan could not be more on point. And what worries me is how relentless the narrative battle has to be. Because the only place where I would disagree with Bryan is, I think, out of the Civil Rights Movement: we won the narrative battle . . . ish. And by that, I mean two things. One, there were a lot of compromises on the narrative: It's all about, you had to be peaceful, and love, and "content of character," and "I have a dream," right? So that's distorted, number one. Number two: you never really win the narrative. You have to keep it up. And I can remember when I first came to the Legal Defense Fund in 1988, Julius Chambers was the Director-Counsel, and I was litigating voting rights cases, and I was getting ready to file a case in Oklahoma, and I had my little press release. And I remember Julius—noble, brilliant civil rights lawyer, whom I revered—saying,

"We do our talking in the courtroom." Which is kind of a nice thing to say.

But actually, that was precisely the moment when the Heritage Foundation and American Enterprise Institute were forming their centers, and they were creating a narrative and a story. I can remember when I started teaching constitutional law—you get your casebooks and so forth. And back in the eighties, to use the words reverse discrimination to describe affirmative action was like a slur. You couldn't call affirmative action reverse discrimination. By the time I was in my seventh year of teaching, the Rotunda casebook, the whole section on affirmative action was called "reverse discrimination." So they had taken over the language, because we hadn't tended to it. There was a way in which we won some of the narrative, and then, as you say, we kind of left it alone. And so you have to keep at it. There's no permanent win.

Bryan Stevenson: I think if you don't hold people accountable for the narrative assaults that they make, then you're never going to prevail. Because the South never voted for the Voting Rights Act, or the Civil Rights Act.[3] They regrouped, started organizing in precisely the way you are describing, and then, forty-eight years later, they won a Supreme Court case, *Shelby County*, because their narrative persuaded the United States Supreme Court that we don't need the Voting Rights Act anymore (at a time when we still saw the same suppression efforts). So I agree.

I look at domestic violence. When we were young, there was a show on TV called *The Honeymooners*. And the punchline was Jackie Gleason saying to his wife, "To the moon, Alice," which was a threat of violence. And everybody laughed. We didn't take domestic violence seriously. When women called the police to their homes after being assaulted, the cops would tell

---

3. The Civil Rights Act of 1964 is a piece of federal legislation that outlawed discrimination based on race, color, religion, sex, and national origin in nearly every sphere of American life, including voting, public accommodations, public education, public facilities, and employment.

jokes to the guy to get him calm. As long as he was calm, they wouldn't make arrests. And then we began to work on the narrative. We actually allowed women who are survivors of that violence to have a voice. They made the movie *The Burning Bed*. And we started talking about the pain and the injury and the suffering. Before you knew it, we started to think differently about that. And today, even these elite, professional athletes are risking something—not nearly enough, we still have a long way to go—when they engage in these acts of violence.

I think we've seen the same thing on climate change. But we haven't made that kind of effort on race in my view, to direct things at the communities that need a narrative shift. And I think until we do that, we're not going to make progress. I live in Alabama, and to me, Alabama doesn't look a lot different than it would have looked eighty years ago, from the landscape level. If you're celebrating Jefferson Davis's birthday as a state holiday, if Confederate Memorial Day is a state holiday, if you don't have MLK

Day, but it's "MLK/Robert E. Lee Day," there is a narrative problem in your state. And, our two largest high schools, Robert E. Lee High and Jefferson Davis High—they're 99 percent black, and nobody is saying anything about that. And that's where I believe we've got to begin to re-engage in a conversation that doesn't give away the power of the history; that is why we are all up here talking about race.

Tony Thompson: So let me ask you, if we don't tether that conversation to court cases, how do we make it part of the national discourse, part of the national dialogue?

Loretta Lynch: I think it can start with court cases, in terms of the reactions to the court cases that we are seeing. I think some of the biggest disappointments for me have been this administration's change in how they're dealing with transgender issues. And I agree with both of you on the importance and the power of the narrative. When you shift away from this concept of taking away entitlement from one group and giving it to another, and focus on the pain that groups feel—groups that are actually all alike—you can start to shift that narrative. And that's what we've started to do with our focus on transgender and LGBTQ rights: focus on the commonality of pain. We're all different, but we can all suffer in similar ways. And so I think when it comes to racial issues also, you're right: the narrative has been hijacked. It has become one of a limited slice of equality being taken from one group to the benefit of another who has not worked for it.

But that narrative is as old as the hills. And so I think, when we look at how narratives are successfully changed, you come at them from another way. One of the ways in which you're often able to get success is not by talking frankly about what's right or what's moral, but by talking about the cost of something. The cost of racism in this society to everyone—the literal dollar cost of racism to GDP—is huge. It's tremendous. And so one way to engage on those issues, I think, is to expand the discussion beyond the whole moral issue. You have a group of people who at this point are probably not going to change their minds on that.

So look instead at how these issues harm this country. You know, we're losing people, people disappear. We're losing the benefit of people who could contribute to society. That's dollars and cents. And that actually has been the way that we've been able to cross over and bring certain groups into discussions like criminal justice reform, that you never thought you were going to get those groups into. What will happen with that, I don't know. But I think also expanding the narrative beyond what people expect to hear, and focusing on the commonality of the pain it's causing all of us, is a way to start.

Sherrilyn Ifill: One of the things that worries me actually goes to Derrick Bell and interest convergence; and it is that when we assign the dollar value to it, when we say, "We should behave in certain ways because this is what it costs us"—I think it's an essential part of the conversation, but I worry that it covers over some of the truth-telling that is part of the narrative that Bryan is talking about. Because it makes our pursuit of justice and equality about pragmatism, and not about moral rights or wrongs, or justice, or the rule of law, or the things that I think have the real staying power, because I think people are remaking calculations all the time.

On the other hand, I do agree that dealing with the economics of it is something that we have also failed to do, and frankly, it's part of the narrative. Next year will be the fiftieth anniversary of the Fair Housing Act, and we're planning all these things around housing because housing discrimination and housing segregation are huge parts of what constrains economic mobility and opportunity in this country.[4] The actual landscape of America shows us the ways in which

---

4. The Fair Housing Act (FHA) of 1968, as amended, bars discrimination in the sale, rental, and financing of dwellings based on race, color, religion, sex, national origin, disability, or familial status.

America has invested in creating what we see today. And I say that to people all the time: we accept the physical landscape as though it is inevitable, and not as though it was created by a series of decisions and investments.

Unpeeling that narrative of equality and investments, I think, is really important. When people say to me, "My family never had slaves," or "We were always nice people; we're not implicated in any of this," I just find it to be really astonishing. I mean, here we are, all in the same country; you move into a neighborhood, you turn on the water, water comes out of the pipe. Your grandparents didn't make the pipes in that city, but you accept the water that comes out of the pipe.

There are all these ways in which we accept the advantages of wherever we are. You come to this country, your parents or your grandparents are immigrants—we all still have a cookout on Memorial Day, even though your parents or grandparents didn't serve in World War II, we do all these things. We take all the benefits! All the good memories. All the things that make us great.

But when it comes to the other part of the history, that also is part of our history that we have to take responsibility for, whether it's lynching, or whether it's the fact that part of the reason that you were able to live the life that you live is because this country decided, after World War II, to make a massive investment in creating the white middle class. They did it through the GI Bill, through billions of dollars of the interstate highway system that allowed suburbs to be made, that created this world that we think of when we want to "make America great" again. It's like Wally and the Beaver and all that stuff. And all of that was created by massive investments—things that were not available for black people, because it was not to create the *black* suburbs. And even if you were a black GI, you couldn't move into *any* neighborhood, you couldn't buy a house in *any* neighborhood. The FHA, once they started insuring mortgages in the 1930s, created red-lining and would not allow integrated neighborhoods.

Loretta Lynch: And these were all government programs . . .

Sherrilyn Ifill: And these were all government programs! So to the extent you're harkening your mind back to some lovelier time, you need to understand that that time was constructed. And I'm not even saying, "Let's deconstruct it." I'm saying, we have the power, with investments, to make the society we want to make. In the 1950s, we decided to make it, and we made it. We made something that everybody recognizes—the winding road, the cul-de-sac, the interstate highway, the Levittowns (that wouldn't let black people live there, but got all the tax development breaks), and so forth. Let's suppose we took a different tack today. Let's suppose we wanted to create a society in which we limited the disparities in equality, in which people had access to housing, access to homes, in which there was rapid transportation outside of New York City and other big cities. We could do it. The same way we did what we did in the 1950s! So my piece is to get people to understand that it's not just about feelings. It's about investments, and investments follow your direction as a society.

Tony Thompson: How do we get these issues as part of the national discourse? Bryan, your TED talk has been viewed 5 million times worldwide. So there's interest in the discussion of injustice and race. But we don't have it in a sustained way. How do we have that conversation in a real, sustained way in this country?

Bryan Stevenson: I think it builds on what Sherrilyn was just describing. I listen to what she just said, and I want to say to the U.S. government, and particularly to the United States military— you *owe* something to black veterans in this country that you have not paid. You owe something. My dad just died a couple weeks ago. He was a vet; he fought in the Korean War; he tried to build a house in 1958—it cost $12,000. He was still paying for that house in 2017, because he couldn't get the loans that his white comrades got when they came back from Korea. And there are tens, hundreds of thousands of people just like him! And now, I'm going to have to, with my siblings, deal with that debt. And I'll be honest, I'm angry at the United States military. Because they didn't do for black veterans what they should have.

Families like mine didn't get into the middle class. We were low income. We were poor. My parents said "low-income but upper class," and I went with that, and I took it as far as I could go . . . which wasn't very far! But I think there's an institutional demand that we should be making. So my organization has been doing this work about the lynching and terrorism that black veterans confronted when they came back from World War II. Many of them were lynched and murdered just because they were wearing the uniform. And we haven't talked about it. So I want to say to the U.S. military, what should you do for this generation of black veterans, to whom you owe something, whom you have not paid? So I think we have to talk institutionally.

Then I think we have to talk socioculturally. The thing I'm fascinated with right now, is that *Alabama's constitution still prohibits black and white kids from going to school together.* It is in the state constitution. And the only way you can get it out of the state constitution is to have a statewide referendum, where people vote on whether to remove that segregation language out of the constitution. We have tried twice now to get that language removed. In 2004, 52 percent of the people in the state voted to keep the language in the state constitution. In 2012, after the election of Barack Obama, the number went *up* to 63 percent.

Here's the bizarre thing: nothing in Alabama generates more unqualified pride than our college football teams. Our teams are serious. Alabama, Auburn, they are no joke. They win. They won a bunch of national championships, and it's probably the thing about which there is more enthusiasm, more community, more excite-

ment, than anything in that state. But I look at
that team. They were in the national champion-
ship this year. It's a predominantly black team.
In fact, at times it's an *all* black team. And if
you said to those football players, "What you're
doing is unconstitutional"—if you said to people
in Alabama, "You can't have that football team
until you change this constitution," all of a sud-
den there's going to be a tension that no one cur-
rently feels. A state constitution that bars racial
integration in public universities ought to be
seen as a threat to our dominant college football
programs. And I think we have to create that tension. If players being recruited posed questions
about the state constitutional ban on integration
we'd reassess the cost of our silence about the
legacy and continuation of racial bigotry.

Sherrilyn Ifill: That's what I meant about the
cost of racism to everybody. That's a cost to
the pride of Alabama. (You're right; football is
a religion.) So I've been thinking about this,
what I call the equality dividend. Have we ever

calculated the benefit? I speak to all kinds of groups, and I very often speak to extremely successful and wealthy people in the hopes that they will support the Legal Defense Fund with some money. I take great pride in speaking to these groups, because I feel very confident that in almost every room full of successful people I'm in, the NAACP Legal Defense Fund had a role in making that room. Just because of the work that we've done.

But what I wonder is, have we been going about it the wrong way? Have we failed to calculate the money that gets made and has been made off the reputation of a country that was created and constructed by civil rights activists? What you could say about America in 1950 is very different than what you could say about it in 1955. You walk into a room in 1960, 1965, and you're a businessperson, and you carry with you this idea of America as a place of democracy, a place where the rule of law reigns, a place of equality, a place of opportunity.

There is—or was—a kind of moral superiority to being an American in many places in the world. That had a tremendous benefit to this country. It allowed us to be who we were in the Cold War, and to—some would say—win it.

But we've never calculated the equality dividend. It's like for free. We just made America look really good. Because the truth is that America was confronted with the most marginalized people in their society, who stood up and said "no more," and confronted that inequality, and did it without guns, and without fists, for the most part. They stood up and confronted the most powerful country in the world. And to its credit, the most powerful country in the world didn't kill them all. Didn't do it! Killed some. But didn't kill them all. And instead made some effort to transform itself around the things that we think of as the pillars of the Civil Rights Movement. And if we're honest about it, that's true. And that's a source of pride in this country.

So what's that worth? We just give that away for free and make it like you did us a favor? We did America a favor, by creating and constructing that identity, which is the identity people really are advancing when they talk about America as a place of equality and justice. It's an identity that we really helped construct.

Bryan Stevenson: But one of the challenges is that when you are oppressed, or enslaved, and you're finally emancipated, you don't feel like you have space to hold people accountable for your enslavement. When you're dealing with terrorism and lynching, you don't feel like you have space to hold people accountable for that terrorism. When we get into the Civil Rights Era, each period in our history, we have been struggling with these forces that are so over-whelming, that even when we get on the other side of the force, we don't feel empowered to say, wait a minute, let's talk honestly about this . . .

Loretta Lynch: But I also think that we feel that having won the legal battle, we've won the over-all war. And the reality is, we did change a lot of laws. And you're right; people did it, if you think about what happened in the fifties and sixties in this country, when we were young. They did it by going to different places and sitting down. They sat down. And who would have ever thought that that would literally have changed this country and the world. But we thought that that was the war. And that was only the battle. Because those beliefs were still there. And those beliefs continue. I hold no answers to how we parse the human heart and get rid of racism, except to basically make it not worth anyone's while. To engage in that . . . that's what works.

Tony Thompson: Loretta, you and I have been talking a little bit about how we have those conversations at a local level. And I think it's one thing to hold this government's feet to the fire, but I think it's another thing to build a movement that reimagines democracy from the ground up. How do we do that?

Loretta Lynch: I think people are beginning to recognize that we have to do that now. My predecessor, Attorney General Holder, is working on a project on redistricting and looking at the issue of gerrymandering in this country, and how that has not only suppressed a lot of voices, but how, at the local level, it can be dealt with, and hopefully reversed. That's the kind of individual local empowerment that has to happen. This all starts at the local level. It starts with somebody believing, "I can run for city council." And realizing that they can, in fact, not just win and be the black face on the city council, the female face, the LGBT face—but that they can actually get something done. And that they can, in fact, wield power.

We have to focus on growing the next group of people who are going to join the political discourse, and in fact wield that power at a local level. I think it's important, because we were blessed for eight years. We had a wonderful president. He will go down in history as one of our greatest presidents. I was tremendously proud to work for him. But politics is about more than who the president is. Law enforcement is about more than who the Attorney General is. It's so much more than that.

What we were trying to do is to travel across the country and empower local voices, to highlight people who are dealing with these issues in communities at the grassroots level. And we were trying to lift their voices up, amplify them, and share them with the nation. Those voices are still out there. And those are the ones that we have to count on at this point in time. Because you can in fact make change at a local level. You absolutely can.

I've spent several weeks in North Carolina lately, and they're trying to come up with a compromise to the HB2 bill banning transgender people from bathrooms.[5] Whether they will or not, the economic boycotts have led that state to realize that it must change. And it's been at

---

5. Passed in 2016, North Carolina's House Bill 2 ("HB2") struck down all lesbian, gay, bisexual, and transgender anti-discrimination laws across the state, and required that in government buildings, individuals use only the public restrooms that correspond with the sex identified on their birth certificates.

the city level—it's been discussed at city councils, at the statehouse, and all throughout that state. And we have to recognize that all politics is local, as one of our great leaders said. It all starts there. And if we want to rebuild to the point where we do have a federal government that is responsive to our needs, and that does listen to people, and is based on inclusion, not fear and exclusion, we have to populate it with people who hold those values dear, and we have to cultivate those people now.

Bryan Stevenson: I appreciate that, but I just don't want to leave the law part out, because it's a critical component. Because the truth is we have a framework where the narrative ought to work for us. We talk about equality, rights, justice—we have all of that out there. These are guaranteed rights. But they don't get enforced. And so that's where the law part comes in. And I don't want anyone to think that that's not going to be a critical component of how we move forward.

There was never a time in the county where I grew up where black children would have been permitted to go to public schools if it was left to a vote. The majority of people in that county were always going to vote for racial segregation. It took a court decision enforced by lawyers from the Legal Defense Fund, coming into our community saying, "No, you have to open up the public schools to kids like Bryan Stevenson." But for that intervention, I wouldn't be here today.

And that use of the law to push the society to confront its obligations is really key. We don't have marriage equality in this country because we won the narrative battle writ large. The narrative battle helped us get the court to do the right thing. But we won it because of the legal decision that now creates that option. And so we've actually got to be prepared to represent those local leaders when they step out and say, "I want to do something;" when those college football players say, "I'm not going to play for this team if we don't do something about this."

There's got to be some group that's prepared to stand up and support them. Dr. King and Rosa Parks were supported by lawyers who got them out of jail, who advanced their mission.

And that's where I also worry, that we haven't created the kind of legal infrastructure that is prepared to do the push work, the narrative work that has to be done. Sherrilyn got involved in a case twenty or thirty years ago, where there was an effort made to try to create great remedies for the survivors of the Tulsa riots—the horrific racial violence that took place in 1921. We've got survivors of racial violence all over this country. You know, segregation wasn't just "direction." There were signs that said white and colored, but those weren't directions. They were assaults. People got injured by that. My parents were humiliated every day of their lives. And we don't really have the extensive infrastructure that we need to represent those people.

So I do think we're going to have to radicalize our sense of what it means to be a civil rights lawyer. You can't just be waiting until something really extreme happens. You've got to get in there, and work with community groups, and people who are trying to make a difference— have their backs, as it were. And then be prepared to be smart, tactical, and strategic.

And I want to emphasize that last word, because one of the problems we have when we start talking about race is that we don't always want to act strategically. And we don't win when we don't act strategically. It's frustrating to act strategically, because you don't get to say what you want when you want it. You have to say it at the right time and in the right way. And that's painful at times. But we need more strategic litigation to actually create the environment. What Sherrilyn and the Legal Defense Fund are doing in Texas is critical to whether we regain voting rights in this country. It's a strategic intervention in a state where there are critical needs. And I just think we've got too few lawyers, too few law institutions, too few people thinking about how we are going to become architects. Charles Hamilton Houston said to graduates of Howard

Law School, way back in the day, "When you graduate from this law school, you're either a social engineer or you're a parasite." I don't think it's a crazy thing to be saying anymore. I really don't.

Tony Thompson: Loretta was a great ally as we moved forward on the Civil Rights front. Now we're not going to have those allies in the federal government. Sherrilyn, who are your partners going to be, and how should we think of partners when we're pursuing this legal strategy?

Sherrilyn Ifill: I have to remind myself all the time that it was just eight years that Obama was president. And before that, the partnership was not great. So I just think we shouldn't get it twisted, like we've had this unbroken line of standing shoulder to shoulder with the federal government—not really! We have to remind ourselves of that. When I was a young lawyer at the Legal Defense Fund, that was not the case.

It was not great. So we should just remind ourselves of our own power.

Let's take policing reform. That's one of the areas in which I've been the most exercised and agitated. And I've said to people that you have taken for granted what happened over the last four years. When the next conflagration happens, the next uprising, there will not be Eric Holder flying to Ferguson to be in the coffee shop and shake people's hands. There will not be Loretta Lynch to fly to Baltimore and sit around a table with community leaders in the midst of the unrest. That's not going to happen. So what's going to happen? You know what Jeff Sessions is going to be saying: he's going to be talking about "law and order." And they want the police officers to have all the military equipment. And God knows what President Trump will be tweeting. All of this is going to fan the fires. So it's deeply problematic.

And we're not going to have these pattern-and-practice investigations. But we should also remember that again, under the Obama administration, pattern-and-practice investigations doubled. Before that, we didn't have a lot of them. What did we have? Well, think about one of the places that's really led on creating the narrative and moving forward the whole issue of policing reform: New York City. No pattern-and-practice investigation from the Justice Department. No federal intervention at all. How did it happen? A ten-year campaign that included strategic communications, organizing, an extraordinary group of activists on the ground, and litigation challenging stop-and-frisk. We filed one of the stop-and-frisk cases in public housing. And all of those came together in that case that went before Judge Scheindlin, that ended up with a consent decree, that in some measure helped move Mayor de Blasio into office. It changed the whole dynamic.

Look, let's be clear. Twenty years ago, there was not the phrase "stop-and-frisk." That was created through strategic communications around a campaign designed to address the issue of police brutality in New York. And it did not happen because we were in a partnership with the federal government.

So I only say that to remind ourselves that *we can do it.* But it requires an extraordinary amount of resources, a lot of time, and it took all of those elements: the litigation, organizing on the ground with activists, and an extraordinary communication strategy, working in concert toward a common strategic goal. So that means that we can do it in other places as well. I would say when it comes to policing, you know, New York is as tough a nut to crack as any place! New York is tough on this issue and has been at it for a very long time. So I think reminding ourselves of that power is important.

The only other thing I want to say is about local power, which Loretta began to refer to. When I was a lawyer at the Legal Defense Fund as a young person, I remember we got a call to do a voting rights case in Galveston, which we ended up taking on. But when I first heard about the case—it was a case challenging the way justices of the peace and constables are elected—I didn't know why this was an issue, or why people were so exercised about not being able to elect black justices of the peace. (I'm a New Yorker; I thought justices of the peace were the nice people who married you when you eloped, like I saw on TV.) But going into the community and learning the police power that justices of the peace have, the control they have over tickets—all the stuff you see in Ferguson and so forth—I understood how important these local offices are.

One of the things we do at the Legal Defense Fund is, although we do challenge the state of Texas's voter ID law, and the state of Alabama's voter ID law, and no doubt we'll be involved in redistricting and so forth, a lot of the voting rights work we do is at the local level. We're going to trial in two weeks, in Terrebonne Parish, Louisiana, challenging the way judges are elected there. It's really looking at the county commissions, the water boards, the school boards, the town council, the railroad commission, the sheriff—the sheriff! I mean, we try to really get down into the nitty-gritty of how political power is constructed and controlled in this country.

And the problem with those of us who very often are in New York and are shiny and want to be civil rights lawyers is that we don't want to go to Etowah County, Alabama, and challenge the way county commissioners are elected. And I think part of the issue we have to talk about is geography: it's a big country. All the civil rights lawyers can't be here in New York. And they can't all be in California.

Bryan and I serve on boards together, and Bryan can shut down any meeting. People start talking about wonderful new innovations. They'll start telling us about what they do in Seattle, and New York, and in New Hampshire. And I look at Bryan, and I know he's getting ready to blow. It sounds so wonderful: "This is what we did in San Something California." And then Bryan just drops the A-bomb—the Alabama bomb. "What are you going to do in Alabama?" Because at the end of the day, this is what we've written off—"they're all red states, and they're all down there, and if we could just get these blue ones in the middle!" But 50 percent of black people live in the South! You are writing off most black people when you decide that you don't want to deal with the issues of the South.

Loretta Lynch: And you're missing opportunities to provide real power to real people in ways that affect lives very, very directly. The school board in most communities determines curriculum. They determine teacher tenure, the makeup of the schools, the school experience of children, all of our children . . .

Sherrilyn Ifill: But the school board in Texas adopted that textbook that was being used all over the country, that tells lies about American history.

Tony Thompson: So let me talk to you all about education, since we brought that up. I want to give you some numbers. What we've generally done is we've looked at different pathways out of inequality. We've looked at education, as one of the primary pathways. But recently, education has been a pipeline to the criminal justice system. I'm going to give you some numbers from the U.S. Department of Education, Civil Rights office:

- Black students account for 18 percent of the country's pre-K enrollment, but make up 40 percent of preschools' out-of-school suspensions.
- Black students in K–12 were expelled at three times the rate of white students.
- Black girls were suspended at higher rates than any other girls and most boys.
- A quarter of the schools with the highest percentage of black and Latino students did not offer Algebra 2.
- And 1 in 5 girls of color with disabilities received an out-of-school suspension.

How are we going to begin to have a conversation about the disparate treatment of children of color?

Bryan Stevenson: I think it reflects the same problem that we've been talking about. And I hate when I go to colleges and give talks. It pains me to say it, but I have to say it: at every school I go to, I say to the kids of color, it doesn't matter how smart you are, how hardworking you are, how talented you are, how much kindness you have in your heart. If you're black or brown in this country, you will go places where you're going to be presumed dangerous and guilty. There is a presumption of danger and guilt that follows black and brown people. And it is most insidious for children. Because they show up, and they don't know how to overcome a presumption of dangerousness and guilt. They're just four and five, trying to live their lives! But we've allowed that presumption to manifest itself.

I think we have to step back again, and start

asking bigger questions. We have a lot of school districts where there are children who are in real stress. You know, you've got two hundred zip codes in this country where the overwhelming majority of the children are expected to go to jail or prison. I think that's a health crisis. I really do. I think the Centers for Disease Control should declare a state of emergency in those zip codes. Because we've got children born to violent families, living in violent neighborhoods, going to violent schools. When they show up at four and five, they have trauma disorders that we're not diagnosing or treating. When you've got a trauma disorder, what you need to do is to make the child feel safe, but we do the opposite. We threaten them. We make them go through metal detectors. We've got teachers who sound like correctional officers, principals who sound like wardens. And then we demonize these children.

I think we have to step back and say, "Who are these children and what do they need?" What do these communities need? And I think education, at this point in our history for these really high-stress communities, has to partner with medical and mental health. Because we've got a medical crisis in these communities. I sit down with twelve- and thirteen-year-old boys who tell me that they don't expect to be free or alive by the time they're twenty-five. And they're not saying that based on something they've seen on TV. That's what they're seeing in their world. And if we don't engage those children in a different way, we're not going to make them understand the things they need to know.

I think we have to change some of the metrics. I don't think the Department of Education should be giving high scores and awards and all of this stuff to these schools based on their test score performances. I think they need to make suspension and expulsion one of the metrics that we use to grade schools. And I think if you have a high suspension rate and a high expulsion rate, you are not a good school. If we made that one of the primary metrics, then those schools would have to figure out, well, how do we help these kids? How do we keep them in school? How do we keep them from being suspended? How do we keep them from being expelled? But we haven't done that. I don't think it would be that hard with the right leadership, to persuade someone. That's a real priority if we want to change things.

Sherrilyn Ifill: Bryan is just spot on. And I think the thing that prevents us from doing that is that we are caught in the grip of a kind of bizarre nostalgia. And I think we have to break ourselves out of it. It may be that this period we're in right now with this administration will cure us forever, but it's a kind of nostalgia, right? We want schools to go back to "the way they were." We want policing to go back to "the way it was." No. No!

We actually have to let public services meet the public; define what are the parameters of good public service by the way in which that service *serves* the public. I hear people say, as teachers, "I'm not a social worker." Well, maybe now you kind of have to be a little bit of a social worker. Or we need to have social workers embedded in schools.

I'm fascinated by and obsessed at this moment with thinking about the resources that exist in communities. Because resources don't just come from the sky. If we're going to build from the ground up, I need to know, what's there already? What do I know, if I drive long enough, I'm going to run into? The school. The police department. And the library. I'm a big library person, because it's already there. And how do we transform those institutions to become institutions that are truly responsive to the needs of those communities? When I was on the board of the library in Baltimore, we got tired of hearing about all these people working on food desert issues in Baltimore. So one of the things we did was to create a food program in the library. You could order online, and you pick up the produce on Tuesday in your local branch. Because we knew the library was in every community. So, sure we want to get a

Giant. Sure we want a SuperFresh. But until then, you could go to the library and get the produce.

In terms of the schools, part of what I think is the problem is that these metrics that Bryan is talking about are supposed to get us back to some period when we think that school was really "great," instead of transforming the schoolhouse to be a locus in the community that provides all the things that children need—counselors, social workers, physical activity, parent learning classes in the evening, all the meals that you need, the instruction—in a kind of one-stop shop. That's what we need for the twenty-first century: to give those children a future, to educate them, to salvage their families, to give them a place of release from trauma.

You know, I'm the youngest of ten kids. I loved school. I loved it! You went to a place, and you could just do your thing. And it was fantastic! School is supposed to be a refuge from the chaos of your home—not more chaos. So we should be creating that. And the reason I raise the policing thing is I think it's the same thing. The president named that taskforce "21st Century Policing" because of what police officers need to do *now*.[6] What are the qualities you need in a good police officer? Take down the picture of the SWAT helicopter and the black truck on the recruitment brochure. What we need are people who are excellent communicators. People who know how to talk down a situation. People with intact egos. But instead, we think that we're going to harken back to some period when it was Officer Krupke. That's not going to happen anymore. We need twenty-first century police. And I think that's the problem with education that produces those statistics. It's them trying to muscle little black girls and boys into being who they're supposed to be based on this old image of what school is.

---

6. In December 2014, President Barack Obama commissioned the eleven-member Task Force on Twenty-First-Century Policing to "identify best policing practices and offer recommendations on how those practices can promote effective crime reduction while building public trust."

Loretta Lynch: As we bemoan the loss of the last eight years, though, we can't forget the gains and lessons that came out of them. Because a lot of what we're talking about got started during those years. And it can be continued; it can be carried on. It was very deliberately placed in communities, to break down the silos and try to bring people together. On the issue of policing, it was community policing. It was engaging with officers who will say to you, on any given day, "I am more of a social worker than a cop, and that's my job." And they actually love that part of the job. Trying to raise those officers up, as opposed to the ones who themselves have been traumatized and take it out on other people. Recognizing the trauma in law enforcement also is something that has to continue.

I think we also have to think about and focus on continuing the empowerment of local communities, and their voices, in these issues. Local communities are still responsive. People have to demand better. They do. They have to ask for better; they have to demand better. They have to say, "We deserve a school board that looks like us," and elect it. They have to say, "We deserve a police department that knows our kids and understands who they are, and works with us." They have to demand it, and they have to go to City Hall and get it. And that kind of local empowerment I think is what we have to focus on. Frankly I think it's a continual thing, now more than ever.

But those lessons are there. And so I think we can look at the work that we did at the Justice Department, and you're right, these are likely not going to be the pattern-and-practice cases that we saw over the last eight years. But the lessons learned from those cases are tremendous. Communities now realize, "I have a say in how police get trained. I have a voice, I can use that voice." That is a constant drumbeat. Because it's not just that black and brown kids are told that you're dangerous and marginalized. They're also told, "You're stupid." It doesn't matter where you are. It doesn't matter if you make it to the gifted or talented. It doesn't matter if you make it to Harvard. They are told, "You are intellectually less than the person sitting next to you." We have to counter that narrative within every child from day one.

Bryan Stevenson: Oh absolutely. Even if we have things go the way we're describing that they'll go, there's going to be this transition period where young kids are going to be at risk, they're going to be threatened with jail and detention, all these things. And I think the challenge for young lawyers and law students who are interacting with these populations—I think it's important for us, as advocates, as lawyers, as people who represent these children, parents, and communities, to start giving voice to these realities.

If you're a traumatized child and you go to school, and people are just threatening you, and you've never had a moment where you can actually live with some sense of freedom and self, and someone gives you a drug at eight years old, and you use that drug, and for the first four hours in your life, you're feeling the absence of threat and menace, what are you going to want when that drug wears off? You're going to want more of that drug. And we're going to criminalize you for that. And when that child becomes ten or eleven, and they're being threatened and menaced all the time, and someone says, "You know what, join my gang, man. We'll protect you," what we're going to do is actually punish you more, because you made the same choice that anybody else would make if they were living that kind of life. But we haven't given voice to those choices. We haven't actually contextualized these lives. And then we allow legislators and other people to beat up on these drug-addicted children, and these young kids joining gangs, in ways that I think is just completely incompatible with what it takes to actually move us forward.

That's partly all these big issues, but it's also partly these small issues—what we say and don't say when we're standing up for people, standing with people. And I couldn't agree more. When we were at Harvard, Loretta, Tony, and I, I remember not wanting anybody in law school to know that I started my education in a colored school. I didn't want people to know that I was the great-grandson of enslaved people, because I thought it might diminish me. And then I got to a point where I realized that that's actually not my weakness, that's my strength! And then I got to the point where I had to tell everybody!

Tony Thompson: And he did!

Bryan Stevenson: But that transformation is rooted in understanding who we are, and how we got to be where we are, and then giving voice to it. And I don't think we're doing that enough. Even as lawyers representing clients coming from communities that are dealing with these issues.

Tony Thompson: We talked about children feeling inferior, and I know from the folks that come to my office at the law school, and some of the lawyers that I talk to sometimes in those firms and in law school classrooms, that they feel that way. And you need to resist it in the way that we're talking about. We also talked about communities. We're in the midst of the largest migration in history—or at least in the last century and a half—back to cities. This presents some profound problems about gentrification and segregation. How should we be thinking about developing our inner city so we maintain some of our power, and some of the educational power that we're talking about? How do we face those challenges when we think of inequality in cities?

Sherrilyn Ifill: Well, I feel this quite keenly. It's important. It's very complicated, because it raises a cluster of issues that we're increasingly, internally at the Legal Defense Fund, talking about in a kind of a little module around strengthening African American communities—holding on to some of the ability to remain in cities and be able to thrive.

I want to leave education to the side, because I really want to be talking about what is *around* the educational institution, what is around the school. So it's about housing: housing segregation, discrimination, and affordable housing, which is a huge problem in this country. It's about infrastructure, which includes both things like water—and we can talk about that—but also includes public transportation. Again, once you get out of New York and San Francisco you've got to start talking about what the lack of rapid transportation means for people. It creates debt. People have cars who shouldn't have cars, and this is not something I really realized until I left New York and moved to Baltimore. Some of these second-tier cities don't have this kind of transportation, and therefore people don't have the mobility.

Johns Hopkins will hire you in Baltimore. Johns Hopkins is one of the places that hires ex-offenders, to their credit. But to get to Hopkins Bayview on the East side, if you live on the West side where Freddie Gray lived, it is going to take you an hour and fifteen minutes on the bus, even though it's a seventeen-minute ride. There is no rapid transit that connects the African American community that lives East, to West in Baltimore, to the jobs and to that kind of mobility, that allows them to move to different neighborhoods, that allows them to have access to the jobs and so forth. So the issue of public transportation is huge, and it bedevils me, because you cannot do public transportation without serious federal dollars. You can talk local all you want, but unless you have all those good federal dollars, it doesn't happen.

So there's the transportation issue, there's housing, there's the infrastructure/water issue and all of the environmental justice issues that go along with it, and then it really is about how you allow people who live in communities already to hold on. We have a case right now challenging the tax foreclosure procedures in Detroit. Tens of thousands of people lose their homes in tax foreclosures based on a tax system that basically overcharges poor people using a formula from before the 2008 housing crisis, and then people can't pay. If you want to challenge it, you have to show up to the office, one day a month, only during business hours—all kinds of things. So just beginning to drill down and look at how people lose their homes is important. How do people find that they can't live in the city anymore?

I grew up in New York, the youngest of ten kids. How did we make it? We made it because there was all of this public apparatus that allowed our family to make it and to survive. With that thirty-five-cent token, I could have a job up in Harlem, which I did at some point, even though I lived in Queens. You could get around the city. You had City University of New York, and I have a brother and a sister who both attended. Registration was $85 a semester, and that was tough for us to get to $85. But you could do it. So there was this strong investment in public life.

And one of the narratives that has been successfully advanced over the last thirty years is the privatization of almost everything in public life. Whether it's prisons, universities, K–12 schools, everybody wants to sit in their car and drive—it's all taking us away from public life. And public life is the only way that you can keep a strong middle class, the only way that people move from lower socioeconomic conditions into the middle class. The only way you maintain stability is if you have public institutions, public infrastructure, public services that are there to support your life and family.

So, one of the narratives I hope we'll begin to attend to is to reclaim the word "public." And the reason I think it's a piece of what you're talking about, Bryan, is because the word public only became dirty when it became associated with being black. Public housing was built for white people initially. There was nothing about public transportation that was considered black. Public schools—when you think public schools, we know what we're talking about—right?

So we took these things that were pillars of public life and American life, and we racialized them. And then once we racialized them, we could demonize them, and we could starve them of funds. And so now, in Maryland, you can get lots of money to build a highway, but the governor cancels the plan to build a subway in Baltimore that's going to take people to their jobs, because that's public transportation. And when you say in a speech in Maryland that you're giving your tax dollars for public transportation in Baltimore, they know what you mean. So reclaiming that narrative about public and private and detaching it from this demonized and racialized context, I think, is one of the most important narrative engagements.

Loretta Lynch: This privatization narrative is actually old. It's been going on since the Social Security Act was passed, and people have been trying to repeal that in one way or another ever since then. And what they always say is, "Let's privatize it in some way. Let's turn that over to the marketplace." And the marketplace is a wonderful thing, but it has crashed more than once, to the detriment of a whole number of people. And so the privatization debate and discussion has continued. One thing I want to throw out there is that we have to learn from what has worked, in terms of how narratives are constructed, how narratives are advanced, and how they eventually flip the discussion. Because they happen in very similar ways. You start out small, and then it sounds innocuous at first, you know, "Private industry can do a great job at whatever it is, and they will be successful." And they only talk about success. They don't talk about the failures of so many businesses, which is part of private life. But in terms of how we've constructed narratives on the success of public institutions, it's not necessarily a dissimilar path.

We should not be afraid to take a page from the book of people who've done this successfully, in particular in terms of communications strategy, in terms of narrative building, and in terms of shaping the discussion. Because there are things that work consistently for a reason, and we don't take advantage of them often enough.

Bryan Stevenson: I think there's something really powerful in claiming the word public as one of the words that becomes incorporated in this move, this demand for racial equity and racial justice. Because without a really strong infrastructure and public services, *all poor people* are going to be disfavored and disadvantaged. And I actually think it's a way of even building some connections that we've needed to build for a long time across groups, between groups.

Sherrilyn Ifill: You said all poor people!

Bryan Stevenson: That's exactly right. When I tell people about the criminal justice system, clients come to me and I say, "Our criminal justice system treats you better if you're rich and guilty than if you're poor and innocent." White poor people understand that just as clearly as black poor people. They have seen their loved ones be wrongly accused or unfairly treated, and they begin to understand that they need public defense to help them, shield them from this kind of threat. But I think we haven't talked enough about that public/private divide and the way it threatens the very movement and narrative that you're describing, which is key to how we move forward. I think it's a really helpful frame as we start building this narrative conversation.

Tony Thompson: I want to talk for a minute about immigration. I'm from a small community in Northern California that is primarily Latino and African American, and the community is in terror right now. We're seeing this demonization of people of color, Mexicans, Muslims, and it's an old song to many of us. What are the lessons that we can learn and teach from the failures and successes of the Civil Rights Movement now, when we see the kinds of executive orders coming out of the White House?

Sherrilyn Ifill: Well, the fact that they're executive orders is very interesting. And it has been actually incredibly painful, I think, for many people in the country to watch this rending of families and this branding of people in all kinds of ways. The good side of it for me has been watching the role of lawyers in this, and watching lawyers come to the fore and be celebrated. People say to me all the time, the ACLU is getting all that money, aren't you upset? I say, "Listen, when people think lawyers are heroes, I'm good. It's fantastic!"

So that's been great to see. In some ways I think it's forcing an important conversation that we need to have, because a lot of people have trafficked on the low in some immigration bashing, including people in our own communities. And so it's really pushed to the fore a conversation that needs to happen in churches, and so forth, about really, who do we want to be vis-à-vis these people who seek to enter this country? If we get this conversation right, we'll engage the unspoken issue about the role that we play in shaping the conditions in other countries that create the need people feel to leave and come here.

When this election happened, there was a little bit of trauma, and we had some conversation and some drinks, and then we said, "We have to get to work." And we talked about the areas that we knew would be affected. We knew that we would not have the Justice Department as a colleague on voting rights, on policing reform, on desegregation cases in the South. We knew all that. One of the things we wanted to be careful about was to make sure that we left bandwidth to engage in issues that are not the primary issues that we deal with, but that we knew would be under attack, because we said, "This is a moment when there can be no daylight between us and any groups that are under attack." So it's one of the reasons that we immediately started to figure out, what do we want to do in the immigration space? I've reached out to the National Council of La Raza,[7] and we've been focusing on the ICE raids, because we think the ICE raids are very

---

7. Now Unidos U.S.

much connected to the whole issue of policing, since there's all this deputizing of police
departments.[8]

We're really trying to come together to cloak
all these issues with our brand. We just finished our brief today on the transgender bath-
room issue. We're just making sure we have
enough bandwidth in the organization that
we're forming a seamless wall. We don't pre-
tend that immigration is our expertise, but we
said, "We've got to learn something, gotta get
up to speed, and we have to figure out how we
can contribute something." We're not going to
be better than groups that already do it, but we
should figure out what out of the Legal Defense
Fund's brand we can contribute to addressing
that issue.

So that's the space in which we're trying to
operate. It's been quite extraordinary since the

---

8. United States Immigration and Customs Enforcement (ICE) is the federal agency tasked with enforcement of federal laws on border control and
immigration.

election to see—whether it's Planned Parenthood, ACLU, or the Lawyers' Committee—how we really have all stood together. There've been a number of collective meetings about what this moment means, about how we want to deal with the Supreme Court, about the threats that our organizations may be under—I mean it's really been quite encouraging to see this kind of connection. So that's been our approach, to try to leave a little bit of bandwidth so that there's at least a part of every one of these issues that we're bringing into our orbit, and making sure that we play a role in it.

Loretta Lynch: And that I think is the difference that will sustain these movements. And I'm glad you phrased the question that way: What can we learn from the Civil Rights Movement, and maybe from some of the missed opportunities there? I think it was so focused on the immediate issues of the pain of people of color in this country that we were not able to connect them to the pain of other groups in this country.

And it's interesting to me that many of our civil rights leaders had begun to do that when they were cut down. That's where Malcolm was going, when he was cut down, assassinated. He was broadening the appeal of the human rights agenda of the Nation of Islam when he lost his life. That's where MLK Jr. was going too. And people opposed him speaking out on the war in Vietnam. They opposed him speaking out on issues of poverty. And I do think those were missed opportunities. Again, in part because those leaders left us, but also because we were so focused on the immediate and very painful issues of the day facing black people that we did not continue and connect it to the issues facing everyone in this country.

I like how you phrase the narrative now: "We're going to go back to this great time in the fifties when things were great for a certain group of people." But if you look at all the disparate groups that now think that they are going to rise to the top with this narrative, they have as many issues as anybody else. They may be expressed differently, they may come at us in a different way, but the economic issues facing poor people, people of color, people in poverty in Appalachia, in deep pockets of the South—life is as hard for poor whites as it is for poor blacks.

And so we don't bring those groups together. We've let the narrative of racial differences supersede that, and separate those discussions. And I think, when it comes to immigration, we have an opportunity and a challenge to see this as something that could happen to any group, to any one of us. We could be demonized in some way, about where we're from, about our religion. We've seen it in other areas as well. As soon as someone becomes the other, support drops away. Or it becomes sort of vocal, and not the real support that Sherrilyn is talking about. And that's where I think we have to go, not continuing to remain fractured, living in our own heads, our own worlds, and our own issues.

But to me the message of the Civil Rights Movement has always been, *"These are all of our issues. All of us are different. All of us can and* have been marginalized at some time." And I think the issue with immigration is challenging because it's really an economic issue. If you listen to the debate, it is phrased in terms of safety, and economics. You know, "Immigrants are going to make our country and our communities less safe, make people in the streets less safe," or, "They're taking jobs away from Americans." And no one is really drilling down on either of those. We have the facts to dispute all of that. All of that. And we don't use that in the dialogue, in the debate.

Sherrilyn Ifill: I'm a student of Legal Defense Fund history, and one of the things I love is to just mine what I think are some of the things that people don't realize about that history, some of which goes directly to this point. I talk all the time about the fact that the Legal Defense Fund in 1971 won the first sex-discrimination and employment case in the U.S. Supreme Court, and we won that case on behalf of a white woman named Ida Phillips, who had applied for a job at Martin Marietta. It was company policy that they did not hire women who had preschool-age children, because, you know, they should be home taking care of their kids. So when her case was in the Supreme Court, we briefed and argued that case for her, and we won that case.

I think people think about civil rights as something that over here, these black people are doing. And what I always want people to understand is that that kind of equality principle is actually unifying, and essential to unite us all. So Ida Phillips is a white woman, and probably many people who are sitting here don't know that it was the Legal Defense Fund that argued the case that broke this ability of a corporate employer to be able to say, "We won't hire women with preschool-age children."

In the same way the Legal Defense Fund had these strange situations where we would represent people for principles because we understood their otherness—both of the times we represented Muhammad Ali for example. We represented him to get his boxing license back in New York State, and we represented him in the Supreme Court when his draft conviction was thrown out. And it really was about drilling down and understanding: What was the threat that was constituted by Muhammad Ali to the powers that be? And we understood exactly what that threat was. And we understood how it went to this narrative that Bryan was talking about, and how it was relevant to all the other clients that we had in that work.

So being able to see beyond the traditional case that's right in front of you, like the voting rights case, the school board, and being able to make the connections to the way in which oppression works similarly across different boundaries, really can allow you to do your finest work. And it confuses the enemy. It really confuses the other side.

Bryan Stevenson: I also think there's something really helpful in understanding just how we think about group identity, and even personal identity. I've always marveled at the fact that when people think there's some advantage to be gained, they're willing to adopt someone else's identity. "Oh wait, you mean if I'm 1/1000 Native American, I have a better chance at . . . well, that's what I am." In certain sectors, you think that a certain group is advantaged, and you want to be advantaged.

That's not the way this should work. It's actually when groups are being targeted and menaced and threatened and excluded that we all need to get together and say, "We're all Mexican, we're all Muslim, we're all the people." I think one of the lessons from the Civil Rights Movement is that people who were not African Americans stood with African Americans—when they were getting beaten at sit-in counters, when they were getting beaten on the march from Selma to Montgomery—those were the people who were really the allies. Standing after the law has passed, when you're at the White House singing something, that's not so meaningful. But when you're there, engaged in struggle, where people are trying to kill you, and people lost their lives—that's the time when you need to actually stand up and say, "I'm going to be with that group."

Tony Thompson: And we need to make it a collective American problem. My mind keeps going to strategy. We have tended to be so reactive. I want to ask all three of you a question: If we think about one or two most significant weight-bearing walls, when we think about race and inequality and the law, if we were to somehow find a way to knock them down and make progress, what would they be for you? What are the one or two things that you think would be significant as we move forward in this strategy?

Sherrilyn Ifill: Well, I don't have all the answers, obviously. I'll say something really sexy. I'm not going to go top line, "Changing how we feel about . . ." "We all want . . ." I'm not going to say that. My own view is that you change what you can change. And one of the ways that

change can happen in this country is by understanding where dollars go, and by controlling
the money.

We have a very nice and tidy civil rights
statute that is supposed to compel us to watch
where the money goes. And that civil rights statute is the principal reason why people like me
who grew up in New York got bused to an integrated school, and why integration, to the extent
that it happened for a brief period, happened at
all in the North. And that is the Civil Rights
Act of 1964. And the Civil Rights Act of 1964,
in addition to outlawing segregation in public
accommodations and other things, states that
the federal government may not provide funds
to any program that engages in discrimination.
And it was the Civil Rights Act of 1964 and that
prohibition that made Northern schools begin
to desegregate, because they thought they were
going to get the money cut off from the Department of Education. And in very rare cases,
money was cut off. But the threat of it was really
enough. And I'm a big fan of the Civil Rights

Act of 1964. I think it is the most underutilized portion of the statute.

Now, we used to have a private right of action, under Title VI of the Civil Rights Act of 1964, so I could actually sue, until 1997, in a case called *Alexander vs. Sandoval*, when the Supreme Court decided that there is not a private right of action. So if, legislatively, we could get that private right of action back, it would be game changing.

However, even if we don't get it back, the federal government is supposed to, itself, in all of its programs, make an assessment to ensure that it is not giving money to programs that discriminate. Attorney General Lynch knows that this was one of our principal points on policing. We give $2 billion a year to police departments. I never said, "Cut off the money." In fact, I even say "give them more money, if you can," if they can prove that they're not engaged in discrimination.

How do we do that? We have to have the data collection. That means I need to know about diversity, about what kind of training you're doing. The way we challenge the school discipline disparities that we've been talking about is through Title VI complaints that we file with the Department of Education, Office for Civil Rights. That would be the office of civil rights in the Department of Education that the new Secretary of Education Betsy DeVos has said she wants to get "under control."

When we discovered that in Brazos County, the Bryan Independent School District was issuing Class C misdemeanor tickets to high school students for swearing, with a disproportionate effect on black and Latino children, we could file that complaint with the Office for Civil Rights at the Department of Education, and trigger an investigation, because of Title VI. Because you cannot be giving money to that school district if they're engaged in discrimination. They have to do that investigation.

I think Title VI is underutilized. It requires a lot of our resources, because to put together a Title VI complaint is as good as putting together a complaint as though you were going to litigate. Then it requires staying on top of the particular agency, and it's really hard, even when they're trying. Even over the last eight years, when they *were* trying. It's getting the regional offices; it's getting the right training; it's knowing what metrics to use. But it is gold if we could just polish it and reveal it and use it.

Tony Thompson: So Bryan, what would be your weight-bearing wall?

Bryan Stevenson: Well, it's sort of funny. We're doing this cultural work, and for me it's been very energizing, because I went to South Africa, and what I experienced there was that people insisted on making sure I understood the damage that was done by apartheid. When I talked to Rwandans, you can't spend time in Rwanda without them telling you about all of the damage done by the genocide. I go to Berlin, and you can't go a hundred meters without seeing those markers and monuments that have been placed near the homes of Jewish families that were abducted during the Holocaust. The Germans want you to go to the Berlin Holocaust Memorial.

And then I come to this country, and *we don't talk about slavery.* We don't talk about lynching. We don't talk about segregation. And so, our project is really trying to create a new landscape. I never thought during my law practice that I'd be spending so much time working on a museum, but our museum is called "From Enslavement to Mass Incarceration." We have to get people to understand the damage that was done to this country with this legacy. We kidnapped 12 million Africans. Kidnapped them. Brought them across the ocean in this torturous journey. Killed millions of them. Held them in captivity for centuries. And we haven't acted as though we did anything wrong.

We must increase a consciousness of wrongdoing: lynching over four thousand people, taking black people out of their homes, burning them alive, hanging them from trees, brutalizing them, causing one of the largest mass migrations in the history of the world, when 6 million black people fled the American South for the North and West as refugees and exiles from terror. And then segregation: saying to black children every day, "You can't go to school because you're black. You can't vote because you're black." And we haven't really developed any shame about this history.

So what I want to do is, I want to increase the shame index of America. Because we do a lot of things great—we do sports, we do all that stuff. But we don't do mistake very well. We don't apologize very well. And if you don't learn to be shameful about shameful misbehavior, you'll keep doing that behavior over and over again. I think if you say, "I'm sorry," it doesn't make you weak, it makes you strong. You show me two people who've been in love for fifty years, and I'll show you two people who've learned how to apologize to one another when they get into trouble.

I think we have to create that cultural moment where apologizing becomes okay.

And part of the reason why we don't want to talk about this history, is we've become such a punitive society. Most people think, well, if we talk about slavery, lynching, segregation, someone is going to have to get punished. And I just want to say to people, "I don't have any interest in punishing America for its past." I represent people who have done really terrible things. I'm not interested in prioritizing punishment. I want to liberate us. I want to get to the point where we can say, "That was bad and that was wrong and we need to get to someplace that's better!" I want to deal with this smog created by our history of racial inequality, so we can all breathe something healthy, feel something healthy.

And so for me, the big barrier is to create a cultural moment where we start talking about this history, where we start putting up markers at every lynching site. Where we start reclaiming the narrative around what happened around that era of segregation. Where we start talking about slavery. There are slavery spots in New

York City that haven't been acknowledged and recognized.

When I go through the Holocaust Museum, I walk through it, and I'm shaken. And what I say is, "never again." We need to create places in this country where you come and you have an experience with the history of slavery and lynching and segregation, and when you come out you say, "never again." And if we get enough people in this country to say "never again" to this history of racism and bigotry, we won't be facing some of the problems we're facing right now.

Loretta Lynch: Bryan started at the root of so many of the problems that we have here, which is how we see each other. But looking at what we actually can change, the load-bearing wall for me I think would be continuing to push for significant criminal justice reform. I've been a prosecutor for over twenty years, and what you prosecute and how you prosecute defines you as a society. It tells communities, families, and the world whom you value and what you value. It tells people what their status is. Are you a victim or are you a perpetrator? I've had cases where I've had people who could be either one on any given day. And so how we handle people who are caught up—as my grandfather used to say— in the clutches of the law, I think reveals a lot about who we are as a society.

And, like Bryan too, the stories about your family that you used to never tell, and now you tell everyone: my grandfather was a sharecropper and a minister. He had eight children and a third-rate education. He'd built a church next to his house. When black people in his rural North Carolina community got in trouble, they would come to him, and he would hide them from the sheriff, who knew him, and who probably knew what he was doing.

My grandfather was a righteous man; he was a moral man. He was a man of conviction in God. But for him this was a bigger issue, because he knew that if there was no fairness in how people were treated, then there was no justice for anybody in that community. So, when I look at our criminal justice system and the years that I've spent working in it, I do believe that it exists to protect people, and I was very proud to be able to protect many communities who'd never had anyone to protect them.

But looking at the way in which we choose how we punish and whom we punish is fundamental to who we are. And I still actually have a sliver of hope. Because I think by enlarging that debate people can see the human cost, and the moral cost—the cost to race relations in this country, but also the economic cost, which translates into other kinds of harm. Think about the things that we could be doing, and could be investing in, other than locking up people who are not necessarily the problem. And I'm not saying that there aren't people out there who are problematic. Again, I have a very realistic view of human behavior and what we need to do to hold people accountable. But layering on the things that we have layered on—adding those issues of fear: "I'm afraid of you and therefore it's much more likely that I'm going to lock you up."

When you lock people up in this country, they're forgotten. And I think the reason we were able to get to a point where we almost succeeded with reform is that we've now locked up so many people, from so many backgrounds, you know, what was the number now? It's like, *a quarter of Americans* have been touched by the criminal justice system in their life. If not that person, then a family member or a friend. So now, everyone is seeing how it can drag you down and keep you from living up to your full potential. So we were able to get a cross-section of people who for a variety of reasons realized that we had to focus on being more effective, more efficient, and more fair.

Tony Thompson: So let me ask you guys one last question each. After the election, with the uptick in religious and racial violence in recent weeks, a lot of young people have lost hope. We've been through this before. Sherrilyn swears she wasn't born during that time, but we've been through this before. How do you keep a sense of hope and optimism, given what's happened and what we've seen?

Sherrilyn Ifill: So this has nothing to do with the law. I talked about this in my church just yesterday, actually. About remembering. About how much power we get from remembering. My own view is that we have very, very short memories. And we really need to engage an understanding of the people who came before us, and what they actually had to overcome. And I'm not even just talking about black people. Because really, the world has come apart time and again over hundreds of years.

And if you're sitting in this room, it means you come from a line of people who were able to survive whatever they had to survive at some point. You weren't always this wealthy and didn't always look this good and smart. Someone, somewhere in your line, had to overcome poverty or war or famine or devastation, or terrible health, or injustice. And I think our dis-connection from those stories is so deep that we sometimes think we can't survive what we can survive.

So I talked about a woman in my church because I was interviewing her—she was eighty-five at the time I think. I was writing my book about lynching, and I was asking her if she had been alive when there was a particular trial of someone who was accused of murder, who was almost lynched in this Maryland town. And we were talking about something else, and she said, "I was the first black poll worker in this town." And she described how she was the first black poll worker when she was sixteen. Her father wanted the polls watched, but he and his male colleagues, African American colleagues, knew that if they went into the polling place, it would be seen as threatening. So he thought that his daughter and her friend were smart enough that they could do it. He got them a bag lunch, and they observed the polls all day.

So I was talking to Ms. Valerie, and it was so

inspiring to me, because here we were wringing our hands—Can we challenge voter ID? What can we do?—and this sixteen-year-old girl was a poll watcher in the 1940s. And I think we just need to connect ourselves to those struggles. Some of the struggles will make you say, "never again." Some of the struggles will expose you to the realities of human nature that we really have to be aware of, and not engage in magical thinking. But some of it tells us about our power.

I talk about Thurgood Marshall, and challenging segregation at University of Oklahoma Law School in the *Sipuel Fisher* case. First day of trial, he and Ada Sipuel, who is the African American woman who's applied to University of Oklahoma Law School, are sitting at a counsel table, and he's trying the case. Well, it had never occurred to them that they could not eat in the cafeteria of the courthouse. So at the end of the day he laughs, and he says, "Tomorrow, I'll try the case, and you bring the bologna sandwiches." Ha ha ha. Very light-hearted. And I love it, because he always wore it very lightly. Right? I would march on Washington because I want to eat in the cafeteria. I try to remember Marshall and try to do that myself—wear it lightly.

But it also tells you something about what it means to have your "eyes on the prize," and to be able to see something that doesn't exist for you. So he cannot eat in the cafeteria, but he is trying this case that ends up in the Supreme Court—which he wins—challenging segregation at University of Oklahoma. And it tells you something about how you have to have your eyes focused further on the horizon, rather than just on what's in front of you.

These are difficult times. One of the things I'm very much against is people pretending that we're not in trouble. We are in trouble in this country. I think we're going to make it. But it's going to require us really being serious about the moment that we're in and being serious about how we're going to get ourselves out of it. I know we can do it because of what's happened in the past, and we *have* to draw on that. We *have* to draw on that history. We have to draw on that determination. We have to draw on that strength.

I mean, I just told you about Ida Phillips. Why would this woman take this case to the Supreme Court? I find her so fascinating. Who wants to work at Martin Marietta? This is the kind of determination that people were able to show. This is the kind of determination that I see in my clients all the time. So my hope really comes from them, from people about whom you have to wonder, why would they do it? Why not just "go along to get along?" But they don't. They say, "I'm willing to sign on the line." They're Barbara Johns, who walked out of Moton High School in 1951 in Prince Edward County and really forced the Legal Defense Fund to file the Virginia *Brown* case before we were ready. Her principal said, "Don't do it, don't walk out. Don't create this problem." And she said, "I have to do it." She just had a building dedicated to her in Virginia by Governor McAuliffe last week. A sixteen-year-old girl.

So it's those people. If you're channeling them, then you *have* to be hopeful, and you have to be optimistic.

Tony Thompson: Professor Stevenson?

Bryan Stevenson: Well, I think Sherrilyn said it. We have to understand who we are in this struggle, in this story. I get overwhelmed a lot of times. We've had a lot of tough days, doing what I do. Just came here today, and the state is seeking another execution date. And every now and then I go into the front part of the office and I look out the window, and I think about the people who were trying to do what I'm doing sixty years ago. And what they had to say frequently is, "My head is bloodied but not bowed." I've never had to say that. And it just tells me: I don't get to complain.

This is probably not the best way to say it, but you don't have the choice of being hopeless. It's just not even a debate you should be having with yourself. You don't get to be hopeless, and then call yourself someone who's trying to do justice. You just don't. And that's what Thurgood Marshall understood. He understood, I can't be hopeless and worry about that. Hopelessness is the enemy of justice. When you are fighting for justice you are fighting against hopelessness. Injustice prevails where hopelessness persists. So you have to see hopelessness as a kind of toxin that will kill your ability to make a difference. And the truth is, you're either hopeful working toward justice, or you're the problem. There's nothing in between. You can't be neutral. No, you're part of the problem.

I absolutely believe in looking back and understanding that you're standing on the shoulders of people. I really do think that sometimes when you feel worried, and you're not sure you can do something, push yourself! Be the person who stands up when everybody else sits down. Be the person who speaks when everybody else says, "be quiet." And you'll find a power in being that voice, in being that light, that representative, which will make clear to you that you can do so much more than you think you can do.

I couldn't agree more with what Sherrilyn said. My grandmother was the daughter of people who were enslaved. I tell this story a lot. I was a little boy, and my grandmother used to squeeze me so tight I thought she was trying to hurt me. And then I would see her an hour later and my grandmother would turn to me and she'd say, "Bryan, do you still feel me hugging you?" And if I said no, she would jump on me again. And by the time I was ten, she'd taught me and all the other grandchildren, as soon as we'd see our grandmother, the first thing we would say is "Mama, I'll always feel you hugging me." And she had this way of creating a relationship to you that would never end.

When my grandmother was in her nineties, she was still working as a domestic, she fell on a bus, she broke her hip, she developed cancer, she was dying and I went to see her. I was holding her hand, last time I was going to see her. I knew she was going to pass away soon. I thought she was asleep, I thought she wasn't listening. I was sitting there holding her hands, and I said something to her, and then I said goodbye, and then she squeezed my hand. The last thing my grandmother said to me, she said, "Do you still feel me hugging you?"

And there are times, right now, in the midst of a lot of conflict and controversy, when I will feel that extraordinary black woman who wrapped me up in her arms, hugging me. And it's through that kind of strength, that kind of witness, that I do not have the choice of becoming hopeless. And I believe that if she could fight the way she fought, I've got to fight even harder and even better. That's what I do for hope.

Loretta Lynch: I could obviously echo those sentiments all night. But I think the challenge I hear you raising is for young people today: our college students, law students, people who are starting out, and who for the last eight years have really seen the best of America. They've seen America rise to a better place. I don't want to imply that we were finished. And now it sort of feels like, not just a reversal, but literally going backward, to a time that a lot of them really can't fathom, can't really focus on, because it's not their world. It's not their reality.

And I know that the reason why it is so important to raise up our history is because if you don't, it just becomes a story. You don't understand what it means, and you don't understand that Bryan's grandmother, the daughter of slaves, probably in her world, was just a working woman holding her family together, but instead was an inspirational figure. Or that the plaintiffs that went to the Legal Defense Fund way back in the forties or fifties viewed themselves as average ordinary people without anything special about them, but have become very special. That's why history is important.

Going forward, I say to young people when they raise this issue that these are difficult times, and you're going to see some things that are going to shock you, stun you, scare you. Maybe you've seen them already. They're going to make you wonder, what has America chosen, and why? They're going to make you wonder, can we survive all of this?

All that will happen. But they will also make you look at yourself in a way you never thought possible. They will make you figure out what's important to you, whether it's an issue, or a cause, or a personal concern. The times we are in and are about to transition through will highlight what's important to you in ways that you can't see right now. And you will find the issue or the cause that touches you. You'll find the issue that's most meaningful to you, whether it's immigrant rights, or human rights. Whether it is criminal justice reform, or being a civil rights lawyer, or whether it's politics. It'll come to you. And it'll come to you in ways that you can't imagine right now. And it's going to be painful to get there, but it always has been. This is hard work. It has always been hard work. But it is the best work that you will ever do—the work of bending your shoulder, and making this world a little bit better, in whatever way comes to you.

It is the best thing you'll ever do; it'll make you the best person you will ever be. And so that's what I see ahead for young people today. That's my hope.

Postscript

The nation's mood since the 2016 national election has been largely one of despair, with good reason. The early signals emanating from the capital raise genuine concern that this administration will look to reverse many of the gains we have made in human rights and social justice. So, it is perhaps expected that this conversation reflects and acknowledges some of the anguish we feel. But the welcome surprise is the profoundly positive tone. In the midst of our disappointment and unease with where we find ourselves, we hear both hope and the building blocks of our agenda going forward.

We are still only beginning to measure and

understand the seismic changes at the federal level. Given the upheaval in Washington, an understandable reaction might have been to throw up our hands or to sit in stunned silence. But this conversation reminds us that we cannot sit idly by or give up on the federal government. Instead, we must wage our battles legislatively and in federal courtrooms throughout the country to hold the line on what we have accomplished. We discuss the pressing need to file lawsuits to protect the hard fought battles of the last decade. Voting rights, employment discrimination based on race, gender, and sexual orientation will continue to be part of our litigation agenda and may become all the more critical given this openly intolerant environment. At the congressional level, we already know some of the key confrontations ahead of us: health care, Planned Parenthood, Medicare, and other lifelines to those who live at the margins. To win these legislative battles, we will find ourselves vying for votes from legislators who traditionally have not supported our communities. To persuade them to vote in ways that protect rather than harm, we will need to use every arrow in our quiver including active participation in protests, town hall meetings, and organizing our communities to let national representatives know the consequences of reversing course.

Our strategy must also concentrate on the local level—in states, cities, and counties. We have an opportunity to push for further gains locally by tapping into the sentiment of those who made up the popular vote in November 2016. It will be important to support the efforts of local officials who are looking to maintain the sanctuary status of cities and are even working to extend the designation to states. If campaign rhetoric proves accurate, we may find that the United States Attorney General may look to pursue policies that we thought had been relegated to the past and, in so doing, may move the Justice Department from ally to adversary. For example, the Department of Justice will likely withdraw its oversight of law enforcement at the local level. So we will need to step in and work collaboratively at the local level to create new remedies for police and community tensions. Those of us who have spent time on the front lines of these battles understand that local victories can be long lasting.

Of course, making sure that our hard won battles have lasting effects is no small task. I hope that we will remember the discussion about the centrality of narrative in moving our agenda forward; our political and legal victories will gain traction only if we tend to the public narrative around race and inequality to ensure that our story does not get hijacked by those in power today. If this election has taught us anything, it has been that winning the battle in the courtroom or in the legislature is not enough; we need to create and manage the public dialogue. The courtroom win and the legislative victory can be fleeting. To make these victories stick and be transformative, we have a duty to help the public understand at a granular level what these battles mean for the lives of people.

The only way to challenge the national narrative and to remind the public what really is at stake is to make room for voices that have not traditionally been part of the political conversation. Our strength and our ability to move a progressive agenda forward lie in engaging those voices in the national conversation. Those individual stories of difficulty, loss, and triumph make up the real narrative of this country's flaws, ideals, and ambitions. We need to include and elevate those voices as we wage our battles for this country's soul. This conversation proved to be so much more than a lament over our current state of affairs; rather, in it we have seen the beginnings of a blueprint for a new progressive direction in America. This is a call to arms. We are ready to proceed on the new progressive path because we recognize that by changing the national conversation, we stand to change the direction of a nation.

—Anthony C. Thompson

Acknowledgments

I would like to begin my thanks by acknowledging the profound contributions to equal rights and social justice that Sherrilyn Ifill, Loretta Lynch, and Bryan Stevenson make on a daily basis. This country would face even greater challenges without their vigilance and voices. Because they think deeply about issues of justice, I knew that their participation would be essential to this conversation, and their comments and reflections at a time when many were still at a loss for words helped to rally our audience to recommit to racial and social justice particularly given the urgency of the current political environment.

I would like to thank my team at the Center on Race, Inequality, and the Law, Vincent Southerland and Danisha Edwards, who worked tirelessly to make this event a success. I would also like to acknowledge the strong support by of the dean of New York University School of Law, Trevor Morrison, as well as that of my colleagues, Professor Kenji Yoshino and Professor Kim Taylor-Thompson. I would also like to note the efforts of generations of NYU Law students who have fought for the establishment of a Center on Race, Inequality, and the Law for many years.

Finally, I would like to thank Diane Wachtell and Jed Bickman at The New Press for their support. Diane's progressive vision and encouragement is what led to the publishing of this important and historic conversation at NYU.

Sherrilyn Ifill is the president of the NAACP Legal Defense & Educational Fund (LDF), based in New York City.

Loretta Lynch was the eighty-third attorney general of the United States and lives in Washington, D.C.

Bryan Stevenson is the executive director of the Equal Justice Initiative, based in Montgomery, Alabama, and the author of *Just Mercy*.

Anthony C. Thompson is a professor of clinical law and the faculty director of the Center on Race, Inequality, and the Law at New York University School of Law.

Publishing in the Public Interest

Thank you for reading this book published by The New Press. The New Press is a nonprofit, public interest publisher. New Press books and authors play a crucial role in sparking conversations about the key political and social issues of our day.

We hope you enjoyed this book and that you will stay in touch with The New Press. Here are a few ways to stay up to date with our books, events, and the issues we cover:

- Sign up at www.thenewpress.com /subscribe to receive updates on New

Press authors and issues and to be
notified about local events

- Like us on Facebook: www.facebook
  .com/newpressbooks
- Follow us on Twitter: www.twitter
  .com/thenewpress

Please consider buying New Press books for
yourself; for friends and family; or to donate to
schools, libraries, community centers, prison
libraries, and other organizations involved with
the issues our authors write about.

The New Press is a 501(c)(3) nonprofit organization. You can also support our work with a tax-
deductible gift by visiting www.thenewpress
.com/donate.